DRUGS AND THEIR DANGERS

OPIOIDS AND THEIR DANGERS

by Susan E. Hamen

BrightPoint Press

San Diego, CA

BrightP◇int Press

© 2020 BrightPoint Press, Inc.
An imprint of ReferencePoint Press, Inc.
Printed in the United States

For more information, contact:
BrightPoint Press
PO Box 27779
San Diego, CA 92198
www.BrightPointPress.com

LIBRARY OF CONGRESS CATALOGING-IN-PUBLICATION DATA

Names: Hamen, Susan E., author.
Title: Opioids and their dangers / by Susan E. Hamen.
Description: San Diego, CA : ReferencePoint Press, Inc., [2020] | Series:
   Drugs and their dangers | Includes bibliographical references and index.
Identifiers: LCCN 2019005409 (print) | LCCN 2019007504 (ebook) | ISBN
   9781682827147 (ebook) | ISBN 9781682827130 (hardcover)
Subjects: LCSH: Opioid abuse--Juvenile literature. | Opioids--Juvenile
   literature. | Drug abuse--Juvenile literature.
Classification: LCC RC568.O45 (ebook) | LCC RC568.O45 H3475 2020 (print) |
   DDC 362.29/3--dc23
LC record available at https://lccn.loc.gov/2019005409

CONTENTS

FACT SHEET 4

INTRODUCTION 6
AN UNEXPECTED DEATH

CHAPTER ONE 12
WHAT ARE OPIOIDS?

CHAPTER TWO 22
HOW DO OPIOIDS AFFECT THE BODY?

CHAPTER THREE 40
HOW DO OPIOIDS AFFECT SOCIETY?

CHAPTER FOUR 56
HOW IS OPIOID ADDICTION TREATED?

Glossary 74
Source Notes 75
For Further Research 76
Index 78
Image Credits 79
About the Author 80

FACT SHEET

- Opioids are medications made from morphine. They come from the opium poppy plant.

- Opioids can be highly addictive.

- Opioids work on special receptors in the brain. This causes the user to feel euphoria.

- Opioids can slow breathing and heart rate. An overdose can occur if a user takes too much.

- Users of opioids are more likely to use heroin.

- Overcoming opioid addiction requires treatment.

- Medicated withdrawal is an option for patients.

- Opioid abuse costs the United States almost $78.5 billion a year.

- From 1999 to 2017, nearly 400,000 Americans died from overdosing on opioids.

AN UNEXPECTED DEATH

On April 21, 2016, two members of the staff of recording artist Prince and a medical student found him on the floor of his home's elevator. He was unresponsive. One staff member called 911. When paramedics arrived, they were unable to revive him. Prince was pronounced dead twenty-four minutes after

Opioid addiction affects people from all walks of life, including celebrities.

the 911 call. Police later discovered it was

an accidental overdose. It was the opioid

painkiller fentanyl.

Prince's death shocked the world. He

was only fifty-seven years old. He tried to

live a healthy lifestyle. He avoided illegal drugs and alcohol. Prince exercised and ate healthy foods. But years of performing had taken a toll on his body. His stage acts included high jumps and somersaults. After decades of performing, he had hip pain. He tried surgery. When that did not help, his doctors prescribed painkillers. First was the opioid Percocet. The prescribed amount wasn't enough to relieve the pain. Like many other people, Prince started taking other opioids. Then he started taking more.

Police searched Prince's home. They found prescription opioids there. One of his

Prince's death touched many people. They left memorials at a music venue near his home in Minnesota.

doctors had treated him for hip pain days

before his death. The doctor had prescribed

the opioid oxycodone. But the doctor

wrote the prescription for one of Prince's

staff members. The doctor said he did this

"for Prince's privacy."[1] It's possible that the

Fentanyl has been responsible for many opioid overdoses.

doctor didn't want the pharmacy to know

the prescription was for Prince. Pharmacy

databases track opioid prescriptions. There

is a limit to how much of the drug one

person can receive.

Unfortunately, Prince's story is a common one. Many people who use prescription painkillers become addicted. Opioid use that starts out as pain relief turns to **addiction**. It can lead to overdose and death.

More than two million Americans are addicted to opioids. The number of overdose deaths in 2017 was 47,600. This is more deaths than happened in car accidents. Opioid addiction has become an **epidemic** in the United States. Doctors are working hard with the government to fight the problem.

CHAPTER ONE

WHAT ARE OPIOIDS?

Opioids are strong pain relievers. Opioids include a large number of drugs. Some are legal drugs. They are prescribed by doctors. Others are illegal drugs. Heroin is one example. Misusing any opioid can cause serious health problems. Regular use can lead to addiction.

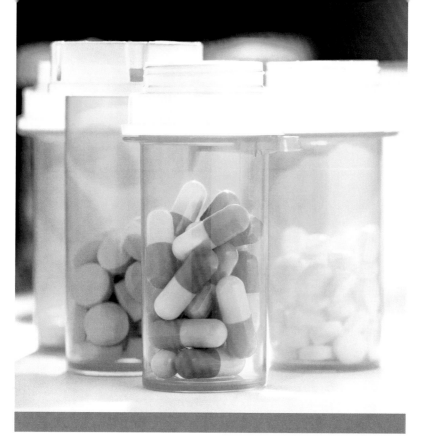

Most opioids are prescription painkillers.

PRESCRIBED USE

Doctors give opioid painkillers for

severe pain. They are used when other

medications don't work. Opioids are often

used to help with pain after surgery.

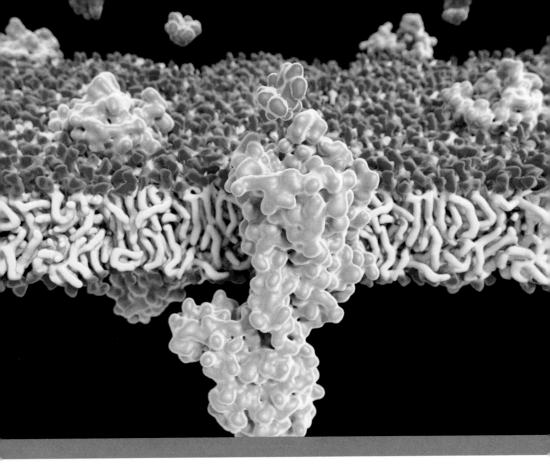

When opioids (red) bind to receptors (purple) in the brain's cell membranes (blue), they can help manage pain.

They can also be used to treat long-term pain. This is called **chronic** pain. They can help cancer patients through the pain of treatments too. Opioids do more than fight pain. They also produce a feeling of pleasure. This feeling makes opioids one of the most misused drugs today.

Opioids are often taken as pills. Oxycodone is one example. Others are used in liquid form. They can be given intravenously. This means they can be given with a needle into a vein. Morphine is given this way.

OPIOIDS AND OPIATES

The class of drugs known as opioids often refers to both opioids and opiates. Opioids are any drug that binds to certain **receptors** in the brain. This is often to help relieve pain. An opiate is made from the opium poppy. It may also be made from chemicals found in or created from the poppy. Opiates can be created using synthetic or natural chemicals. Opiates are opioids.

Some drugs are made using natural and synthetic opioids. These are

---

FAILED DRUG TESTS

Eating poppy seeds has caused people to fail drug tests. The poppy flower has seeds. They have opium in them. They are used for baking. Poppy seeds don't affect people the way opium does. Eating poppy seeds is safe. However, eating them can create a positive result on a drug test.

called semisynthetic. An example is oxycodone. This is used as a pain reliever.

Low doses can help relieve pain. They make users feel sleepy. They can also slow breathing. Higher dosages can cause harmful side effects. When too much is taken, the user may go into a coma or die. Many users experience a sense of pleasure. This is a high. This causes many to continue taking opioids despite their dangerous side effects.

OPIUM POPPIES

Opium poppies grow in Southeast and Southwest Asia, Mexico, and Colombia.

Poppies grow flowers and a large green pod. Inside the pod is a milky, sap-like substance. This is opium. Farmers remove the opium. It is used to produce morphine and codeine.

PAIN MANAGEMENT

Some doctors focus on a specific area of medicine. There are doctors who focus on pain management. They treat a wide range of chronic pain. This could be arthritis, cancer, or chronic neck or back pain. These doctors work to help patients feel better and get back to their lives. They often prescribe therapy or opioids. These doctors are careful to make sure patients don't become addicted.

HISTORY OF OPIOIDS

Opium has a long history. Records from 3400 BCE mention opium growth in lower Mesopotamia. That is modern Iraq. Opium spread until it reached China. Opium was eventually introduced all over the world. In the 1870s, the English researcher C. R. Wright studied the drug. He discovered how to turn opium into heroin. Dr. Alfred Q. McCoy is a professor who studies opium trafficking. He talks about the process of making it: "This final stage . . . requires considerable skill on the part of an underworld chemist."[2] After the discovery,

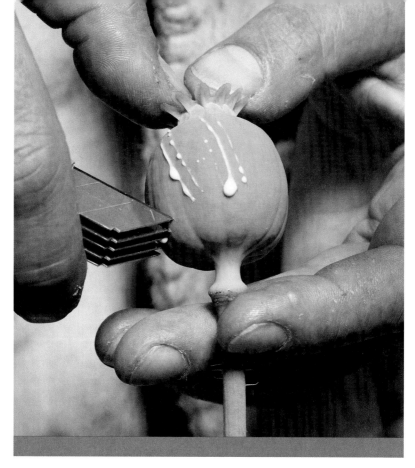

Opium was popular long before opioids such as morphine or oxycodone were invented.

scientists began using opium to create

more drugs.

One of the dangers of opioids is the

belief that they are safe. After all, doctors

prescribe them. However, they are not

always safe. Every user is at risk of overdosing. An overdose happens when the body has too much of a toxic substance. It can lead to serious medical problems or death. When taken incorrectly, opioids can be dangerous. The body begins to build a tolerance to opioids. This means more must be taken to achieve the same response. In the United States, approximately 130 people die every day from overdoses. Researcher Jessica Ho wrote: "The substantial increases in drug overdose mortality that have occurred in the [United States] are both unanticipated and alarming."[3]

CHAPTER TWO

HOW DO OPIOIDS AFFECT THE BODY?

Opioids are some of the most addictive drugs in the world. Opioids relieve pain. They can also cause **euphoria**. This relaxes and calms the user. This feeling is the reason people become addicted.

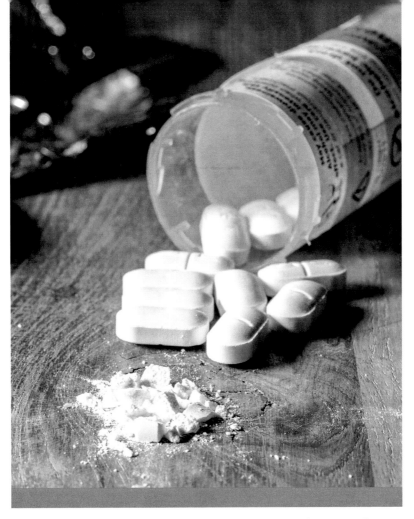

Some users crush pills to snort them. This gets the drug into the bloodstream faster.

Users quickly feel the effects. Once

taken, hydrocodone pills begin working

in ten to twenty minutes. Fentanyl and

Dilaudid work even faster. Some opioid users crush pills. Then they snort the dust. The drug enters the bloodstream quickly. The user feels the effect quickly. But these pills are not meant to be snorted. They are designed to release the medicine into the bloodstream more slowly. When they are snorted, they can cause serious side effects. Users may even die. Morphine given intravenously works much faster than pills. Heroin takes effect almost immediately when injected. The euphoria hits in seconds. Some users feel nausea.

THE EFFECT OF OPIOIDS ON THE BRAIN

The brain has opioid receptors. These are naturally part of the brain. The body produces natural opioids called endorphins. The receptors are activated when opioids bind to them. When the body is in pain or stress, endorphins are released. They bind to the opioid receptors. This prevents the

ABUSE-DETERRENT OPIOID FORMULATIONS

The government is working with scientists to create opioids that are hard to misuse. These are called abuse-deterrent opioids. Some burn the nose if snorted. Others cause headaches if too many are taken.

brain's **neurons** from firing normally. The result is a relief from pain. The person feels better. The endorphins can make a person feel a rush. An endorphin rush is natural, and it is good for the body. It can happen when a person gets hurt. It can also occur when a person is exercising.

When a person takes an opioid, the drug enters the brain. It attaches to opioid receptors. The receptors think the opioids are the natural opioids. The receptors send out signals to activate nerve cells throughout the body. This causes drowsiness and heaviness in the arms

The body releases endorphins when under stress or in pain.

and legs. Thinking becomes hazy. These

effects can last for hours. For a person who

is in extreme pain, these effects are a relief.

But for people who take opioids to feel the

rush, this is called getting high.

Opioids can cause nausea and vomiting. Breathing and heart rate are slowed. With slowed breathing, the user doesn't get much oxygen. This can cause brain damage. The lungs and heart can stop working. This is the response to an overdose. The user may die without immediate medical attention.

MEDICAL CONSEQUENCES

Prescription opioids are useful for pain. They are especially important for easing pain after a surgery. But they carry risks. Only people under the care of a doctor should take opioids. This helps prevent addiction. It also

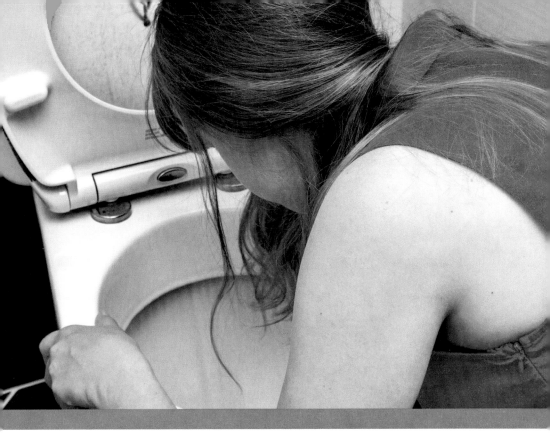

Symptoms of opioid use can include drowsiness and nausea.

helps prevent an overdose. Brain damage

from lack of oxygen can be permanent. This

can lead to short-term memory loss, vision

or hearing loss, and loss of balance. It can

also cause confusion and trouble reading

and writing.

Addiction to opioids happens when a user takes the drugs repeatedly. It can be to get high or relieve pain. When opioids are taken, chemicals flood the brain. This activates a part of the brain that handles reward and pleasure. The brain becomes adjusted to getting large doses. The user begins to crave the euphoria. This leads to misuse. A doctor said of his addiction:

My drug use escalated. In addition to Internet orders I would write prescriptions in the names of my family members. Suddenly, my uncle had knee pain, my father-in-law

PRESCRIPTION TO ADDICTION

Actress Jamie Lee Curtis was addicted to opioids for years. She went through treatment. She has stayed clean for more than twenty years. "Most people who become addicted, like me, do so after a prescription for a painkiller following a medical procedure," she explained.

"Kill the Pain," Huffington Post, *May 5, 2016.*
www.huffingtonpost.com.

back problems, my aunt arthritis. I did not think about the record I was establishing of their purported use, nor did I think about the records of my own prescribing practices. I was out of control, but getting by, taking many pills to get through each day.[4]

When users take more than the prescribed amount, the brain adapts to it. The user needs to take more of the drug to get the same feeling. This is called tolerance.

NONPRESCRIPTION OPIOID USE

Doctors prescribe the minimum amount of an opioid needed to relieve pain. These prescriptions are closely watched. Some states have electronic databases. These systems track drug prescriptions. This keeps people from getting drugs at multiple pharmacies. Some states have created laws to limit the opioids people can receive.

Building a tolerance to opioids leads to addiction. Users who have to take more pills often move to stronger medications or even heroin.

In 2018, Florida passed such a law. It limited opioid prescriptions to three days. For special cases, doctors are allowed to prescribe a seven-day supply. This is for severe pain. The only exceptions are for cancer patients and those with some severe injuries. Such laws limit the amount of opioids people can get. But addiction makes opioid users want more. Some users steal pills. They often target friends and family. They might have started out with a codeine prescription. They will look for any other opioid they can find. This includes fentanyl, oxycodone, and others. Some purchase opioid pills illegally. Some buy fake prescriptions. This is illegal too. Others turn to heroin.

Heroin is incredibly dangerous. Studies show that it can harm brain tissue. This affects a person's decision-making

Switching from prescription opioids to heroin is dangerous. Heroin is an illegal drug.

abilities. It also reduces the ability to control behavior. These changes can be hard to reverse. Heroin use can also cause brain inflammation. This can create symptoms such as confusion and irritability.

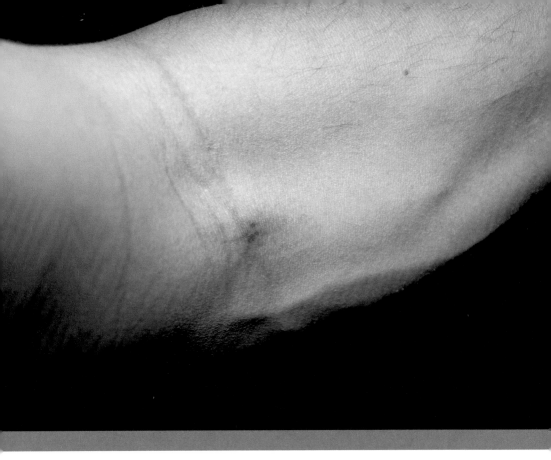

Heroin use leaves marks from the needles.

Injecting heroin can cause damage to the body too. Many heroin users reuse needles. This is not **sanitary**. Bacteria or viruses remain on needles. They can cause infections. Needles also dull with use. Dull, dirty needles leave wounds. The wounds may become inflamed or scarred. These are called track marks.

Heroin also disrupts blood flow. This causes blood clots. Over time, blood clots lead to scar tissue. This stops blood from flowing normally. Blood cannot reach certain parts of the body. This can cause infection. Tissue may die. Users may develop sores. If the area gets bad enough, doctors have to remove it.

ADDICTION

Most people who abuse opioids begin using them for pain. Misuse leads to tolerance. The longer they use it, the more

Addicted users have to keep buying opioids or go into withdrawal.

users need to get high. Eventually, the user

needs the drug to prevent withdrawal. This

is addiction.

Withdrawal is a danger of opioid use.

Withdrawal happens when addicted users

stop taking a drug. Symptoms include muscle and bone pain, vomiting, and more. Users will seek more drugs to stop withdrawal. Dr. Richard Schottenfeld of Yale Medicine says, "You get extraordinarily high **relapse** rates, 85 to 90 percent in a year, and an enormous risk of overdose death."[5] But treatment can help reduce the chances of relapse.

CHAPTER THREE

HOW DO OPIOIDS AFFECT SOCIETY?

O pioid addiction affects all kinds of people. Some babies are born addicted. Their mothers abused opioids during pregnancy. Teens and adults abuse opioids. Celebrities, doctors, and honor roll students have been addicted. About 130 Americans die every day from

Opioid abuse affects all parts of society.

opioid overdose. In 2017, opioids caused about 68 percent of all overdose deaths. Opioid abuse is a public health crisis. It affects the whole society. A survey found that about 11.4 million Americans abused opioids in 2017. The survey counted users

Many teens start abusing opioids. Some addicted users are preteens.

twelve and older. About 11.1 million abused

painkillers or heroin. Of those people, 10.5

million took prescriptions alone. More than

560,000 used prescriptions and heroin. An additional 324,000 only used heroin.

About two million people abused opioids for the first time in 2017. That is an average of more than 5,400 new abusers per day. Roughly one sixth of those are between twelve and eighteen years old.

A GROWING EPIDEMIC

The rise in abuse happened in three waves. It began in the 1990s. At the time, drug companies said that opioids were safe. They claimed the drugs were not addictive. The opioids worked very well. Doctors prescribed more of them. Oxycodone and

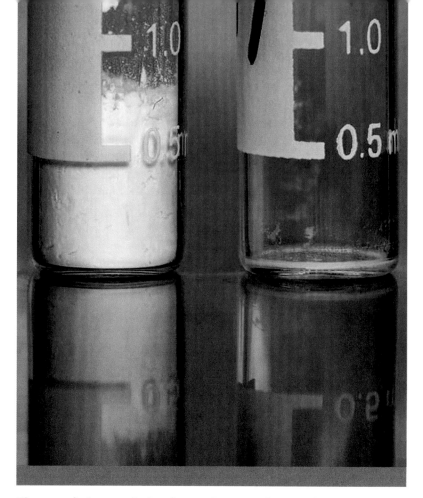

These vials contain drug doses of equal strength. Synthetic opioids (right vial) are much stronger than heroin (left vial).

others became popular. But the number of

overdoses started rising. Dr. Schottenfeld

says, "There was a large-scale

over-prescribing."[6]

Another wave began in 2010. Doctors began seeing a surge of heroin deaths. Painkillers had led many to heroin abuse. Heroin was much cheaper. It was also easier to purchase. Patients wanted more opioids. They bought heroin on the streets.

The third wave began in 2013. This one brought a large number of overdose deaths. Synthetic opioids were the cause. The opioid fentanyl killed many people.

Physicians wrote seventy-six million opioid prescriptions in 1991. That number rose to 255 million in 2012. The total decreased after 2012. But there were still more than 191 million in 2017. Nearly 400,000 people died from opioid overdose from 1999 to 2017. By 2017, 1.7 million Americans were addicted to opioids.

Doctors who prescribe opioids know patients may become addicted. They try to prescribe carefully. But many patients still become addicted. Approximately 21 to 29 percent of patients prescribed opioids for pain abuse them.

DANGERS OF ADDICTION

Abusing opioids over a long period is harmful. The body loses its ability to fight pain. This is because the brain's nerves become covered in opioid molecules. A

simple injury can become painful. The

body can't handle even small pains.

The user then takes more opioids. This

increases addiction.

Physical pain isn't the only problem. The

brain systems affected by opioid use also

PRESCRIPTION PAINKILLERS AND STUDENT ATHLETES

Student athletes are at a high risk of opioid abuse. This is because sports commonly lead to injuries. The *American Journal of Public Health* studied this problem. It found that athletes have a 50 percent higher risk compared to nonathletes. Athletes may need opioids for pain. But they should work closely with their doctors.

Opioid abuse also chemically affects the user's mood.

control emotions. Long-term use of opioids

can make it difficult for a user to experience

normal feelings. This affects friends and

families. Others often notice that users lose

interest in hobbies. They no longer give the user the same joy. Users stop doing many of the things they once liked. This affects users' children too. It's common for users to suffer from depression and anxiety.

HEROIN

About 80 percent of heroin users abused prescription drugs first. The average price of OxyContin from a pharmacy is around $6 per pill. On the street, it may cost up to $80. For some users, this could average more than $70,000 per year. However, a dose of heroin runs $5 to $20. This is much cheaper.

Heroin use has many dangers. Used needles can spread diseases. The needle is contaminated when it touches blood. Hepatitis C and HIV can be spread by sharing needles.

Hepatitis C causes swelling in the liver. Many people don't know they have the virus. They may not have symptoms for a long time. Most of the time hepatitis C is spread by sharing needles. It can be spread by exposed blood too. Users might infect others without knowing they it. Users with the virus have to be careful not to infect others.

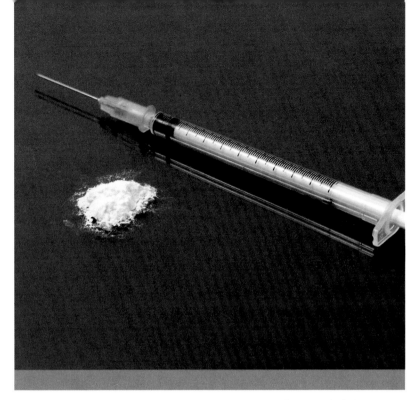

Needles can create new problems for opioid users. Infections can be introduced if needles are reused or shared.

HIV is a virus. It causes the disease AIDS. It is transmitted by blood or other body fluids. When users share needles, HIV can be transferred. Researchers believe that approximately 30 percent of US HIV infections are caused by sharing needles.

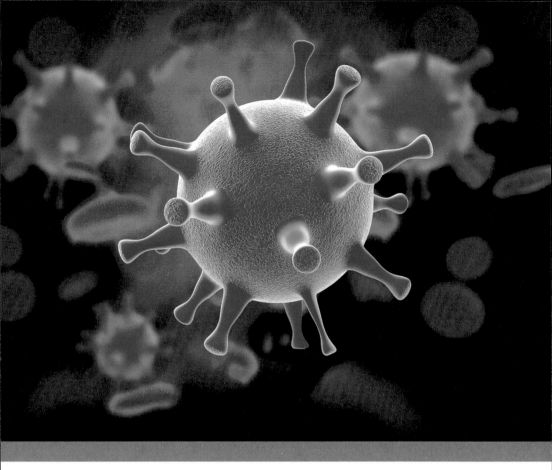

This is HIV. The virus is a real threat for a user who injects drugs. It can destroy a person's immune system.

HIV causes many health problems. There is no cure. If left untreated, it will eventually turn into AIDS. Once a person has AIDS, the body has a hard time fighting infections. The immune system cannot work properly.

RELATIONSHIPS

Opioid abuse affects families and friends.
Users may be unable to have healthy
relationships. They focus on getting drugs.
People around them suffer. Users might
become abusive to partners who try to stop
the users' drug use. Addicted users might
lie. They may become violent. When users
with children are arrested, they often lose
custody because of the drug use.

OTHER PROBLEMS OF ADDICTION

Users can have a hard time working
while high. Once the high has worn off,
withdrawal symptoms start. These can

A runny nose and flu-like withdrawal symptoms can make users uncomfortable. Symptoms peak twenty-four to forty-eight hours after the last dose.

make it hard to work too. A person going

through withdrawal may be too sick to

work. They risk being fired. Seven out

of ten employers deal with employee

opioid addictions. Workers might be absent. Others may work more slowly.

The government studies health issues. It estimates that opioid abuse costs the United States almost $78.5 billion a year. This includes lost productivity in the workplace. It also includes health care and court costs. There are costs for imprisoning users, foster care for children, and more. The opioid epidemic touches everyone.

CHAPTER FOUR

HOW IS OPIOID ADDICTION TREATED?

There are ways to get help. People visit drug treatment centers. Doctors and nurses run these programs. They are trained to help a person overcome opioid addiction. They can also treat the underlying pain.

Medical professionals help patients in treatment centers through withdrawal and recovery.

The first step of treatment is a

detoxification program. It is called detox

for short. During detox, doctors and

nurses help a patient with withdrawal.

They manage the symptoms. They reduce

the dangerous side effects. This is called

medically managed withdrawal. There are

medications to help with opioid detox.

DETOX

Medications help reduce cravings.

Some help prevent withdrawal symptoms.

FIRST RESPONDERS AND NALOXONE

Sometimes paramedics find an overdose victim. They have a medicine to help. Naloxone is an opioid antagonist. It is injected into the body. It restores breathing and heart rate. Naloxone has saved lives. Many states have expanded its use. Some states allow family members of patients to give naloxone too.

They also improve a person's chances of staying in treatment. Three types of medications are used. Agonists activate opioid receptors. Partial agonists do the same thing but produce a smaller response. Antagonists block receptors. This prevents the user from getting high.

Methadone is an agonist. But it does not give the same high as other opioids. It has been used for opioid use disorder since 1947. It blocks opioid effects. One dose can last for days. Methadone works well for people who are severely addicted. Some users eventually wean themselves off methadone. Users will have withdrawal symptoms when they quit. This happens even if they wean themselves down to lower doses. Cristin used methadone. When she quit, she said, "I had withdrawal symptoms for about three months."[7]

Buprenorphine is a partial agonist. It blocks other opioids. It also provides some opioid effects on its own. This helps prevent cravings and withdrawal symptoms. Buprenorphine isn't as strong as methadone. It is used for patients with moderate addictions. It stays in the system for up to sixty hours. Cristin was

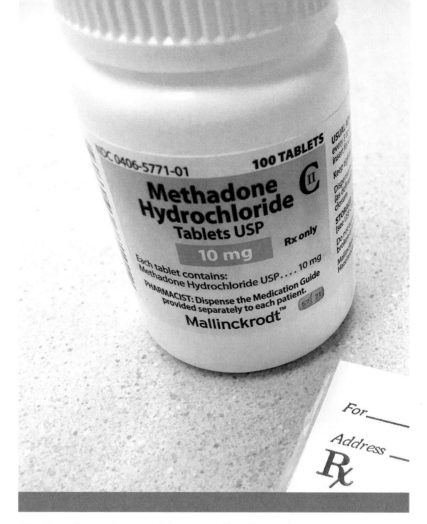

Methadone is used by medical professionals to help patients through withdrawals.

unsure if she could stay clean. Her doctor

recommended buprenorphine. Cristin says,

"It blocks opioids, but doesn't make you

feel sick."[8]

Another prescription is called Naltrexone. It is an antagonist. Naltrexone greatly reduces cravings. Naltrexone also prevents opioids from causing a high. It is often used by people overcoming heroin addiction.

Naltrexone lets patients focus on recovery instead of cravings. It can be taken as a pill or injected. It is also available as an implant. Doctors place it under the skin. The implant works for two months.

Using a prescription drug to help reduce withdrawal and prevent opioid effects is a popular treatment. This is called replacement therapy.

Buprenorphine is a common treatment for patients.

Lofexidine hydrochloride is another medication used. It can be used to make symptoms during detox less intense.

INPATIENT AND OUTPATIENT TREATMENTS

Treatment can occur in an inpatient setting or an outpatient setting.

Inpatient treatment involves staying at a facility. Outpatient treatment works differently. The patient is treated during the day. He or she goes home at night.

Inpatient programs are different lengths. Some research suggests that long programs are best. Ones that last at least ninety days are most effective. Shorter programs carry a higher risk of relapse.

Inpatient treatment involves care from doctors, nurses, and counselors. Patients receive daily therapy. Support groups meet too. Patients undergo cognitive-behavioral therapy (CBT). CBT looks at the connections between thoughts, feelings, and behaviors. It also helps to teach the patient how to recognize opioid abuse. That way, the person can avoid it. Another type of therapy offers patients rewards for remaining clean. This is called contingency

THE TRUTH ABOUT OPIOIDS

At fourteen, Rebekkah was injured. She broke her ankle in cheerleading practice. Rebekkah was prescribed opioids. She became addicted. At twenty-six, she went through treatment. Her rehab was captured on camera. It was for an educational campaign called The Truth About Opioids. "This [opioid] drug addiction has taken everything and everyone I've ever loved away from me," Rebekkah warned.

Quoted in "Rebekkah's Story," Truth, n.d.
www.thetruth.com.

Treatment centers include support groups for patients.

management therapy. It helps encourage people to avoid opioid use.

Many treatment programs include structured routines. Patients get physical exercise. Others use group counseling.

Group counseling helps recovering patients recognize the situations that make them want to use again. They can then better avoid those situations. Some inpatient treatment facilities also offer family therapy. This type of therapy helps a user's family heal as the user does.

Many users have success with outpatient programs. Patients live at home or with a family member. Outpatient treatment is flexible. It allows patients to continue everyday life. Some might have work, school, or family needs. An inpatient program is not possible.

Outpatient treatment programs often offer sessions throughout the day. Patients come to group therapy and support groups. They do other activities that help them overcome addiction. In some programs, patients attend treatment three times a week. This can vary by treatment facility. Patients often start out meeting frequently. They meet less often as recovery continues.

Eventually patients can function without opioids. Many continue with aftercare. They keep meeting with counseling groups. This allows them to receive ongoing help from

Outpatient programs have flexible schedules. This helps people balance treatment with their lives.

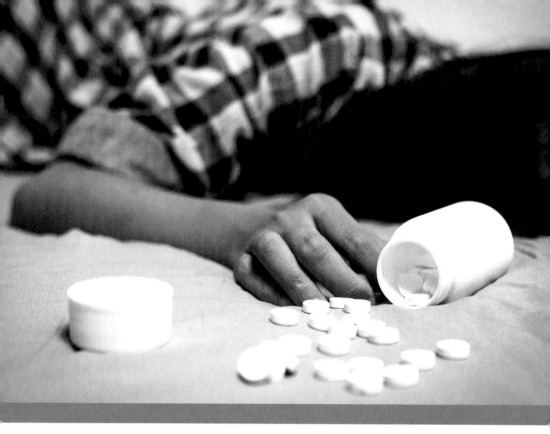

By increasing access to treatment centers, the United States hopes to reduce overdose deaths.

fellow former users. It also lets former users

support newer patients.

GOVERNMENT INVOLVEMENT IN HEROIN REHABILITATION

Addiction is a national issue. In 2017,

the government declared a public

health emergency. President Donald Trump later announced a plan to fight the crisis. The plan included improving access to treatment. It provided paramedics with drugs to treat overdoses. It also funded new pain treatments.

Federal and local governments invest in treatment. Offering cheaper treatment is important. Paying for treatment is less expensive than imprisoning a user. One year in prison costs the government $24,000 per person. Outpatient programs can cost almost $5,000. Inpatient treatment can run as much as $20,000.

THE CONTINUED OPIOID EPIDEMIC

Opioids can help people suffering from chronic pain. Opioid use rose for many years. But there is hope. Those numbers are decreasing. People are aware of the problems. Opioid addiction can happen very easily. It is best to work closely with a doctor. He or she can prescribe the minimum dosage needed.

Imprisoning users is expensive. Funding treatment centers can save taxpayers money.

GLOSSARY

addiction
dependency upon a substance, thing, or activity

chronic
something that lasts for a long time

detoxification
the process by which the body clears itself of drugs

epidemic
a widespread occurrence of a disease within a community

euphoria
a feeling of intense pleasure and happiness

neuron
a cell that transmits nerve impulses

receptor
a cell that transmits a signal to a sensory nerve

relapse
to return to a state of being ill after making some improvement

sanitary
conditions that are clean and sterile

SOURCE NOTES

INTRODUCTION: AN UNEXPECTED DEATH

1. Quoted in Jeff Wheeler, "Doctor Who Treated Prince Agrees to $30k Penalty for Illegal Prescription," *MPR*, April 19, 2018. www.mprnews.org.

CHAPTER ONE: WHAT ARE OPIOIDS?

2. Alfred W. McCoy, Cathleen B. Read, and Leonard P. Adams II, *The Politics of Heroin in Southeast Asia*, New York: Harper & Row, p. 13. 1972.

3. Quoted in German Lopez, "A New Study Shows America's Drug Overdose Crisis Is by Far the Worst Among Wealthy Countries," *Vox*, February 26, 2019. www.vox.com.

CHAPTER TWO: HOW DO OPIOIDS AFFECT THE BODY?

4. "A Personal Story of Addiction," *Massachusetts Medical Society Corporation*, n.d. www.massmed.com.

5. Quoted in Wheeler, "Doctor Who Treated Prince Agrees to $30k Penalty for Illegal Prescription."

CHAPTER THREE: HOW DO OPIOIDS AFFECT SOCIETY?

6. Quoted in Wheeler, "Doctor Who Treated Prince Agrees to $30k Penalty for Illegal Prescription."

CHAPTER FOUR: HOW IS OPIOID ADDICTION TREATED?

7. Quoted in "Overcoming Opioid Addiction: A Woman Shares Her Story," *Yale Medicine*, February 28, 2017. www.yalemedicine.org.

8. Quoted in "Overcoming Opioid Addiction: A Woman Shares Her Story."

FOR FURTHER RESEARCH

BOOKS

Bethany Bryan, *Heroin, Opioid, and Painkiller Abuse*. Buffalo, NY: Rosen
    Publishing, 2019.

Duchess Harris and John L. Hakala, *The Opioid Crisis*. Minneapolis, MN:
    Abdo Publishing, 2019.

Hal Marcovitz, *The Opioid Epidemic*. San Diego, CA: ReferencePoint
    Press, 2018.

Christine Wilcox, *Thinking Critically: Opioid Abuse*. San Diego, CA:
    ReferencePoint Press, 2019.

INTERNET SOURCES

Elissa G. Miller, "Taking Prescription Opioid Pain Medicines Safely."
    KidsHealth, 2018. https://kidshealth.org.

"Heroin and the Opioid Epidemic: From Understanding to Action,"
    Partnership for Drug-Free Kids, n.d. https://drugfree.org.

"Prescription Pain Medications (Opioids)," *National Institute on Drug
    Abuse for Teens*, March 2017. https://teens.drugabuse.gov.

WEBSITES

Department of Health and Human Services
www.hhs.gov

This site contains information and statistics about drug use.

Healthworks! Kids' Museum
https://kidshealth.org

Resources on this site teach kids about the dangers of heroin use.

NIDA for Teens
https://teens.drugabuse.gov

This site answers questions about opioids, misuse, addiction, and more.

Substance Abuse and Mental Health Services Administration
www.samhsa.gov

This site includes information about opioid misuse, its effects on children, and programs to help families affected by opioid misuse.

INDEX

addiction, 11, 12, 28, 30, 31, 34, 37–38, 40, 47, 55, 56, 58, 61–62, 65, 68, 70, 72
AIDS, 51–52

buprenorphine, 60

China, 19
codeine, 18, 34
Colombia, 17

depression, 49
detoxification, 57–59, 62

epidemic, 11, 55

fentanyl, 7, 23, 34, 45

hepatitis C, 50
HIV, 50–52
hydrocodone, 23

lofexidine hydrochloride, 62

Mesopotamia, 19
methadone, 59–60
Mexico, 17
morphine, 15, 18, 24

Naltrexone, 61–62
neurons, 26

opium, 18–20
    poppy, 16–18
overdose, 7, 11, 21, 28, 39, 41, 44–46, 58, 71
oxycodone, 9, 15, 17, 34, 43
OxyContin, 49

painkillers, 7–8, 11, 13, 31, 45, 47

receptors, 15, 25–26, 59
relapse, 39, 64

tolerance, 21, 32, 37–38
track marks, 36
treatment, 14, 31, 39, 56–59, 63–68, 71
    inpatient, 63–67, 71
    outpatient, 64, 67–68, 72

withdrawal, 38, 53–54, 58–60, 62

IMAGE CREDITS

ABOUT THE AUTHOR

Susan E. Hamen has written more than thirty books on various topics for young readers. Some of these include the Wright brothers, the Civil War, and ancient Rome. She lives in Minnesota with her husband, daughter, and son. Together with her family, she loves to travel, play music, and experience new things every chance she can get.